Supporting Details

Level **C**

Book Removed from AAP collection:

Name: _____

Date: _____

One Hundred Passages with Questions for Developing Concentration and the Skill of Recognizing Supporting Details, One of the Six Essential Categories of Comprehension

WALTER PAUK, PH.D.
Director, Reading Research Center
Cornell University

Jamestown Publishers
Providence, Rhode Island

SINGLE SKILLS SERIES
Supporting Details, Level C

Catalog No. SS03
©1985 by
Jamestown Publishers, Inc.

All rights reserved. The contents of this book are protected by the United States Copyright Law. Address all inquiries to Editor, Jamestown Publishers, Post Office Box 9168, Providence, Rhode Island 02940.

Cover and Text Design by
Deborah Hulsey Christie.

Printed in the United States of America

3 4 5 6 7 AL 98 97 96 95 94
ISBN 0-89061-366-4

Preface

Prior knowledge is the key to understanding. For example, have you ever strolled through a museum and wondered why some people were fascinated by an object that looked quite ordinary to you? Prior knowledge gave them the edge. They knew the significance of what they were looking at, and by looking and understanding, they learned even more. And so it is with a page of print. Some people see only words, while others see fascinating meaning.

You, too, can see fascinating meaning in almost all factual writing if you have prior knowledge of these six components: subject matter, main ideas, supporting details, conclusions, clarifying devices, and vocabulary.

By knowing these structural components, it will be relatively easy and highly satisfying to scoop up the meaning of almost any factual passage.

In addition to teaching these all-important components, the *Single Skills Series* does one more essential thing: it teaches concentration. Wrinkled brows, compressed lips, contracted muscles, and held breath won't help anyone to concentrate while reading. Even saying, Concentrate! Concentrate! to oneself is self-defeating, for then you will be concentrating on concentration rather than on the printed word.

The slippery quality of concentration was readily recognized and insightfully expressed by William James:

> Trying to seize concentration is like seizing a spinning top to catch its motion, or trying to turn up the gas light quickly enough to see how the darkness looks.

Though William James identified and described the problem of concentration, he did not come up with a solution; but, we believe, we have. We devised the *anticipation technique,* which is a natural and uncomplicated method, and which is explained in the following pages.

Acknowledgements are now in order. First and uppermost, especial thanks and gratitude go to Robert Strauss. Bob, a writer of a novel, as well as many short stories, not only contributed passages to the series, but also, in a top supervisory capacity, did assist greatly in selecting, refining, and preparing multitudes of passages for final submission to the publisher. In short, he was the in-house editor-in-chief.

I am also eternally grateful to Ross James Quirie Owens, a writer, director, and cinematographer for his contribution of passages, sense of humor, advice, and friendship.

Finally and in high priority, I am indebted to all others who helped. Though not listed in this Preface, they are, nevertheless, inwardly listed and enscrolled forever in my memory.

w. p.
1985

| *Contents*

TO THE INSTRUCTOR 7

TO THE STUDENT 9
   Concentrating
   Supporting Details Lesson

THE STEPS IN A NUTSHELL 13

PASSAGES 14

To the Instructor

The 100 passages in each book of the *Single Skills Series* are designed to help students develop skill in one of the six essential categories of comprehension: subject matter, main idea, supporting details, conclusions, clarifying devices, and vocabulary in context. Built into each reading passage is also a special device that helps students learn how to concentrate, thus comprehend better.

This particular book focuses on the skill of recognizing supporting details. It contains 100 passages, each followed by one multiple-choice question that asks the students to select the answer choice that is a detail given in the passage.

Concentration. To help students develop the skill of concentration, a focusing device employing the *anticipation technique* is used. The last word of each passage is left out. To supply correctly that word, students must continually think while reading. As they read each sentence, they are to try to anticipate what is coming next. By constantly trying to anticipate what is ahead, the students are concentrating. If they have applied this technique throughout a passage, by the time they get to the last word of the last sentence, a word that makes sense in the context of the passage should come to mind. In fact, the exact word that the author intended often comes to mind.

If a word does not automatically come to mind, students have a second chance; immediately following each passage are three words. One is the correct final word for the passage. The other two are decoys. The students, scanning these word choices, should be able to choose immediately the correct word. If they cannot, then they know they were not concentrating carefully enough on what they were reading and that's a signal that they must try harder next time. Each time a student supplies the last word correctly, he or she is rewarded by the good feeling of having succeeded. To keep on getting this reward, students will make concentration a constant reading habit.

Skills Practice. The reading passages in this book are all factual, designed to interest a broad audience of mature readers, and written at a controlled reading level. The readability of each passage was computed by applying Dr. Edward Fry's *Formula for Estimating Readability*.

This book, and every book in the *Single Skills Series*, provides students with one of the most important elements in the learning of any skill: practice. By repeated practice with questions that are focused on a particular reading skill, students will develop an active, searching attitude that will carry over to the reading of other factual material. The skill question in each exercise will help students become aware of the facts and details they are reading at the time they are actually seeing the words on the page. This type of thinking-while-reading helps readers achieve higher comprehension and better retention.

Introducing the Book. For practice to be truly beneficial, students must understand what they are practicing and why. The *To the Student* section of the book provides the basis for the practice. It explains thoroughly supporting details and the part they play in reading material. This section also highlights the importance of concentration and explains the concentration feature of the series. We suggest that you go through this section with your students, making sure that they understand how to do the exercises and how to correct their answers.

Worksheets, Answer Keys and Record Keeping. Students record their answers on reproducible worksheets. There are two different worksheets: one is designed for the main idea questions, each of which requires three answers, and the other is to be used for the remaining five comprehension categories. The answer keys for each grade level and individual student record-keeping sheets are provided for the teacher in convenient reproducible format.

If a student gets most of the comprehension questions wrong for several sessions in a row, have him or her reread the explanation of the skill and the sample exercise at the beginning of the book. Then have him or her reread some of the questions incorrectly answered and, with the correct answers in mind, reread the passages to discover why the correct answers are correct.

When a student answers most of the questions correctly for several sessions, you may want to advance him or her to the book at the next higher level.

To the Student

CONCENTRATING

Do you know that you cannot concentrate on two ideas at the same time? Yes, the mind can bounce back and forth between two ideas. But, like a tennis ball, it can't be on both sides of the court at the same time.

If concentration is ever needed, it is when you read. What a waste of time to have your eyes glide over print while you are thinking about something else! The trick is to tie your attention to what you are doing.

Can you learn to keep your mind on what you are reading? Yes! This book is made to help you do just that. How? By using the *anticipation technique*.

Here's how the technique works: The last word of each passage in this book has been left out. Under the passage are three words. One of these is the correct last word. As you read a passage, you should pick up and hold information in your mind. Use each idea you read to try to guess what's coming next. Do this right up to the end of the last sentence. If you have been truly concentrating, a last word should come instantly to your mind, without your having to look at the three word choices.

After you have thought of a last word, look at the word choices. Quickly choose the one that correctly completes the passage. If you concentrated as you read, you will often find that the word you guessed would be the last word will be the right word choice. Write the last word in the space provided on your answer sheet.

If you cannot easily think of a last word that makes sense when you get to the end of a passage, you will know that you were not concentrating fully. This will tell you that you must try harder on the next passage.

Here's one more tip. To start concentrating, ask yourself, What is this passage about? You will find that by asking this question your mind will be drawn to the writer's words to find an answer.

SUPPORTING DETAILS

Supporting details are just what their name says. They are details that support the main idea of a passage. No passage can consist of only a main idea. It must also have information that explains the main idea.

To many people, the word *detail* means "something unimportant." But supporting details are important. Without them, an idea could not be expressed completely. A writer could not support an argument or a point of view.

Paragraphs are made up mostly of details that support the main idea. The main idea is the most important point that the writer wants to make. A reader must be able to tell the difference between a main idea and supporting details in order to fully understand what he or she is reading.

Keep in mind that supporting details support the main idea. So, if you have trouble finding the main idea of a passage, look closely at each sentence. For each one, ask yourself, Does this support something, or is this the thing being supported?

There are many kinds of supporting details. Some are examples, explanations or descriptions. They may also be definitions, comparisons or contrasts. All of these are used to support ideas.

The passage below shows how important supporting details are for filling out a main idea:

> Ocean water is very salty. All water, even rainwater, has some salt in it. It picks up salt from land and from living things in the sea. But ocean water is 220 times more salty than fresh water. Experts think that there are about 50 quadrillion tons of salts in the sea. If it could all be removed and spread on the earth's land surface, our planet would be covered by a layer of salt more than five hundred feet thick!

The first sentence is a topic sentence. It tells the main idea of the passage: ocean water is very salty. All the other sentences support this idea. In the second and third sentences, we are told that all water has some salt in it. These two sentences lead to the comparison that is made in the fourth sentence. There we are told just how much saltier ocean water is than fresh water. This comparison makes the main idea clearer. It tells us just what is meant by "very salty." The fifth sentence tells us how much salt is in the oceans. And the last sentence contains an illustration that helps us to understand just how much salt that is. By the end of the passage, we have been convinced by all the supporting details that the ocean truly is very salty.

Below is a sample passage and question. As you read, ask yourself, What point is the writer trying to make? Asking this will help you to find the main idea. Try to notice the supporting details as you read. Pay close attention to each idea. When you get to the end of the passage, try to guess what the last word is. Then look at the three word choices that are given. Choose the one that correctly ends the passage. Then answer the supporting detail question. An explanation of the answer choices follows the question. This will help you understand how to think about this type of question.

Bedouins are the wandering tribes of the African deserts. They have some very strict customs related to the roles of men and women. Their ancient culture is based on the Muslim faith. The men may go anywhere they wish. But the women are seldom seen in public. Men and women live in separate sections of their family's tent. Women eat only after the men have had their meal. It is thought to be wrong for women to show their faces, so they wear veils when they go out. It is also thought to be wrong for women to go to school. But a wife often has much to say about how the household is run and how the children are _____.

separated   veiled   raised

Bedouin women wear veils because

(a) they are seldom seen in public.
(b) it is thought wrong for them to show their faces.
(c) they are not allowed to go to school.
(d) they must be protected from the burning desert sun.

Did you concentrate as you read the passage? Then you know that the last word should be *raised*. It is the only word choice that makes sense. Children are not separated or veiled.

The answer to the supporting detail question is *b*. You are told in the passage that Bedouin women must not show their faces when they go out in public, and that that is why they wear veils. The passage does say that the women are seldom seen in public and are not allowed to go to school, but these are not the reasons that they wear veils. So, *a* and *c* are wrong. Nothing is said about the desert sun, so *d* is wrong.

As you read the passages in this book, try to notice the facts and details that you read. If you do this, you will have no trouble answering the questions. Remember, the way to understand what you read is to concentrate!

The Steps in a Nutshell

Here is a quick review of the steps to follow in working your way through the practice passages in this book.

1. ***Concentrate.*** Ask yourself, What is this passage about? just before you begin reading.
2. ***Read Attentively.*** Pay close attention to each idea you read and try to anticipate what will be told next as you go along.
3. ***Fill in the Last Word.*** As soon as you get to the blank at the end of the last sentence, try to think of the word that should go there. Then choose one of the concentration words under the passage as the last word of the sentence. Write that word in the space provided on your answer sheet.
4. ***Answer the Skill Question.*** Read the question and all four answer choices. Mark your answer on your worksheet.
5. ***Correct Your Answers.*** Use the answer key to check your answers. Correct any incorrect answers according to the directions on your worksheet.
6. ***Record Your Progress.*** On your Individual Record Sheet, mark the numbers of the passages you completed, and put an x in the appropriate box for each concentration word or skill question you got wrong.
7. ***Take Corrective Action.*** Look again at the correct answer to each question you answered incorrectly. Then, with that answer in mind, read the passage once more, trying to find out why the correct answer is right.

1 | John Clogg has a rare ability. He can write two different sentences at the same time, one with each hand. Clogg, who comes from England, is being studied by experts. They say he has "double hemisphere action." The two halves of the brain are called hemispheres. Though the two halves are connected, they work separately. Most people use one half at a time. But John Clogg can use both at the same time. So, while most people can do only one thing at a time, John Clogg can do _____.

                four   three   two

The two halves of the brain are called

(a) continents.
(b) hemispheres.
(c) double action.
(d) brains.

2 | The World's Fair was held in New York City in 1964. Many amazing things were shown there. One was the world's largest piece of cheese. It was a huge chunk of cheddar. The cheese weighed more than thirty-four thousand pounds. It was brought to the fair from Wisconsin. That state is well-known for its fine cheese. The giant cheese was much too big to be carried in a car or a plane. It was carried to the Fair on a forty-five-foot tractor trailer called the "Cheese- _____."

           Mobile   **Spread**   **Plane**

The giant cheese came from

(a) New York.
(b) Washington.
(c) Wisconsin.
(d) New England.

3 | Ancient Greek myths say that the first echo was a beautiful young maiden. Echo had only one fault. She talked too much. One of the Greek gods was angered by her constant talking, so he cast a spell on her. After that, Echo could never speak on her own. All she could do was repeat the last words of others. Then Echo fell in love with a handsome young man. His name was Narcissus. But the young man did not love Echo. He loved only himself. Echo became so sad that she faded away, until all that was left of her was her _____.

                smile   voice   eyes

Echo was

(a) a beautiful maiden.
(b) an angry god.
(c) a handsome man.
(d) an evil witch.

4 | Shock and fear can kill a bird. Birds sometimes fly into closed windows. They don't see the glass barrier that is between them and where they want to go. After they hit the glass, they fall to the ground. They are usually stunned or in shock. If someone who wants to help the bird picks it up, it might die. The shock from hitting the window combines with fear when it is picked up. The bird might react by getting so scared that it has a heart attack. So, people who want to help an injured bird should never pick it _____.

                up   down   over

A bird may die from a combination of shock and

(a) germs.
(b) disease.
(c) injury.
(d) fear.

5 | Butter is made from the fat that is in cream. When cream is shaken or churned, the fat comes together. It forms butter granules. After the butter granules have formed, a liquid is left over. This liquid is called buttermilk. The buttermilk is drained off. Next, the butter granules are washed with cold water. Then they are drained and salted. In the final stage, the butter is mixed well. This gives it an even texture and color. People used to churn butter by hand. But today most dairies use machines to make _____.

            milk   butter   cream

Butter is a kind of

(a) fat.
(b) cream.
(c) liquid.
(d) milk.

6 | Trees sometimes grow bumps and knots. These are called galls. They are diseases caused by fungi, worms and bacteria. Galls can grow inside the leaves, branches and bark of trees. Galls are ugly, but they usually aren't dangerous to trees. However, they can kill or stunt the growth of a very young tree. Some people spray their trees to kill the fungi, worms and bacteria that cause galls. But if a gall is big enough to be seen, it's probably too late to stop it from _____.

            branching   growing   budding

Galls can kill

(a) bushes.
(b) wildlife.
(c) old trees.
(d) young trees.

7 | Most large trees have trunks that are about four feet wide. Some trees are much bigger than that. One of the most famous is a giant cypress tree in Mexico. It is called the Zapotec (zahp-uh-TECK) Tree of Life. It stands in front of a church. The tree is so big that it takes forty children to make a ring around it by holding hands. Some scientists believe that this tree is five thousand years old. It is one of the oldest trees on earth. And, at close to thirty-five feet across at the base, it is also one of the _____.

tallest   widest   heaviest

The Zapotec Tree of Life stands in front of a

(a) school.
(b) church.
(c) cliff.
(d) hospital.

8 | Plants need light in order to grow and survive. Most plants rely on light from the sun. But one plant is able to make do with almost no light. It thrives in the dark caves of Europe. The plant is a kind of moss. At the tips of its tiny branches are lens-shaped cells. These cells act as magnifying glasses. The plant magnifies the light in the cave to help itself grow. No cave is completely dark. The moss absorbs tiny amounts of light to use for itself. That way it is able to live and _____.

shine   grow   dim

The moss has special cells that

(a) blossom and flower.
(b) repel insects.
(c) collect water.
(d) magnify light.

9 | Skirts are usually worn by women. But there are two countries where men wear skirts from time to time. The skirts are traditional costumes. The skirts worn in Scotland are known as kilts. Kilts are made from plaid wool. Each Scottish family, or clan, has its own special plaid pattern and colors. So, a plaid kilt shows the clan that a man belongs to. It tells a bit of his history. The guards outside the Greek parliament building also wear kilts. Theirs are white. This is also an old, respected tradition. Men from Scotland and Greece usually wear pants. But for special occasions they wear kilts to honor their countries' long _____.

    traditions   skirts   pants

Scottish kilts are made of

(a) plaid wool.
(b) white wool.
(c) white cotton.
(d) plaid cotton.

10 | Wasps build nests that are a lot like beehives. But wasps don't make honey. They raise young wasps in their nests. Wasp nests have many small compartments. The queen wasp lays one egg in each compartment. Then the worker wasps take care of the eggs. They feed the baby wasps after they break out of their shells. Finally, the young wasps grow up and learn to fly. Then the queen lays more eggs, and the life cycle begins _____.

    again   before   after

Wasps raise their young in

(a) trees.
(b) nests.
(c) lakes.
(d) mountains.

11 | Maple syrup is made from the sap of maple trees. In the late winter and early spring, farmers tap maple trees. First they bore a three-inch hole in the tree trunk. They make this hole about three and a half or four feet up from the ground. Then they put a metal or wooden spout in the hole. They hang a bucket from the spout. Sap drips out of the spout, into the bucket. Once a day the farmers collect the sap. They boil it down in the sap house. After they have boiled away most of the water, they are left with maple _____.

                trees   syrup   holes

Farmers collect maple sap in

(a) holes.
(b) bores.
(c) spouts.
(d) buckets.

12 | Most creatures that have backbones also have a tail. But not all creatures use their tails for the same purpose. Some use their tails as an extra arm. Monkeys use their tails to swing from branch to branch. Cows use their tails as built-in flyswatters. They swish their tails back and forth to keep insects away. The tail on a fish helps it to swim. Foxes use their bushy tails to cover their paws and noses at night to keep them _____.

                cold   warm   windy

Cows use their tails as

(a) flyswatters.
(b) backbones.
(c) extra arms.
(d) propellers

13 | Duck hunting can be awfully easy, as two men found out in 1976. Dr. Ernest Fox and his friend Marshall Trueluck went duck hunting one day. They put out their decoys. Then they hid and waited for the ducks to come. Soon two ducks appeared. They were flying in from opposite directions. The ducks saw the decoys, but probably didn't see each other. They both dove toward the decoys. Then, boom! The two ducks tumbled from the sky. No, the hunters had not fired their guns. The ducks had banged their heads together. They both fell into the water, dead. The two men had found success without firing a single _____.

           decoy   duck   shot

The ducks had dived toward the

(a) water.
(b) hunters.
(c) food.
(d) decoys.

14 | Anteaters don't have any teeth. But they manage to eat a lot of ants anyway. They just don't chew them. Anteaters are well built for eating ants. They have large claws on their front feet. They keep their claws curled up while they walk. But when an anteater is hungry, its claws become helpful tools. It uses them to rip open ant nests. Then the anteater can sweep up ants with its long, sticky tongue and swallow them _____.

           chewed   whole   nests

The anteater has no

(a) claws.
(b) ears.
(c) teeth.
(d) eyes.

15 | Are sharks really killers? People fear that sharks will attack them while they are swimming. But people are more dangerous to sharks than sharks are to people. Thousands of sharks have been killed by humans. Only a handful of humans have been killed by sharks. Sharks do not hunt people. In fact, they try to stay away from humans. If they are frightened, they may kill to defend their homes. Humans are a threat to sharks all over the world. Sharks are hunted in Japan. In Australia and South Africa, sharks are caught and killed in the nets that are supposed to protect swimmers. With people around, sharks have good reason to be _____.

            afraid   friendly   hungry

In Australia and South Africa, sharks are trapped by

(a) swimmers.
(b) nets.
(c) whaling ships.
(d) fishing lines.

16 | There is a group of men in England who throw bricks for sport. Each brick weighs exactly five pounds. That's light enough for most people to lift. But throwing a five pound brick a long distance takes a lot of strength. The champion English brick thrower is Robert Gardner. He once tossed a brick 142½ feet. But brick throwers may soon throw bricks even _____.

            later   shorter   farther

English brick throwers throw bricks that weigh

(a) half a pound.
(b) five pounds.
(c) fifty pounds.
(d) one pound.

17 | People have been kissing for years. But kissing has meant different things at different times. In ancient times, kissing was a sign of respect. In Persia, if one man kissed another on the mouth it was a sign that they were equals. If the kiss was on the cheek, they were not. Christians in the early days used the "holy kiss." It was a sign of friendship and good faith. Kissing didn't become a sign of love until much later. The custom was supposed to have started in France. It soon spread to the other countries in Europe. Today, although people use a kiss as a sign of affection, it still has its older meaning as a sign of _____.

                hatred   respect   war

Kissing was first used to display affection in

(a) the United States.
(b) France.
(c) Persia.
(d) Italy.

18 | Winged moths don't really eat holes in woolen sweaters. By the time moths develop wings, they are at the end of their lives. They lay eggs on wool, fur, rugs and other materials. The eggs hatch into larvae, or caterpillars. These are the insects that eat holes in material. They eat and grow and then spin cocoons. Moths with wings develop in cocoons. But when they come out they don't eat. First they lay eggs, and then they _____.

                eat   die   knit

When moths eat wool they are

(a) winged.
(b) old.
(c) larvae.
(d) cocoons.

19 | Rules were strict in old Pilgrim churches. Older men sat on one side of the church and young men sat on the other. Boys could not sit near girls. Most of the boys sat on the stairs. There was a special guard to make sure that children didn't talk. He also kept an eye on those who seemed to be falling asleep. He carried a long rod to prod children who weren't paying attention. There was a hare's foot on one end and a hare's tail on the other. A girl who was falling asleep would get a gentle brush with the hare's tail. A sleepy boy, on the other hand, got a little rougher treatment. If he looked like he was napping, he got a short rap from the hare's

_____ .

           foot   tail   head

In old Pilgrim churches, boys sat on the

(a) floor.
(b) bench.
(c) stairs.
(d) altar.

20 | Most birds fly fairly close to the ground. They can hunt better that way. Birds catch food from either the ground or the water. They also pick up sticks, twigs and string from the ground to build nests. It usually makes no sense for a bird to fly high. Birds usually fly high only when they migrate to warm places for the winter. They will often fly quite high when they are traveling those long

_____ .

           distances   hunts   places

Birds use sticks, twigs and string to

(a) eat.
(b) find their way.
(c) build their nests.
(d) help them fly.

21 | Have you ever hit your funny bone? Actually, the funny bone doesn't exist. There are three bones in each arm. Two of these bones are in the forearm. The third is in the upper arm. Not one of these is called a funny bone. The funny bone is not a bone at all. It is a nerve that runs along the elbow. Nerves send messages to the brain. They make people aware of what their bodies are feeling. Some nerves enable the body to feel hot and cold. Other nerves send the feelings of pain or pleasure to the brain. When the nerve called the funny bone is bumped, it sends a tingling feeling to the brain. However, if the nerve is hit hard enough, it sends a message of pain to the _____.

brain   leg   bone

The human arm is made up of

(a) one bone.
(b) two bones.
(c) four bones.
(d) three bones.

22 | Some ants can help to heal people's wounds. They are South American leaf-cutters. These ants have huge, strong jaws. South American Indians use the jaws of the ants instead of stitches. If a person gets cut, he gathers some leaf-cutter ants. He holds the ants near the edges of the cut and lets them bite to hold the edges together. Then the Indian pinches off the bodies of the ants. The jaws stay locked to the wound, holding it firmly closed while it _____.

heals   infects   bites

South American Indians use leaf-cutters instead of

(a) food.
(b) stitches.
(c) fuel.
(d) leaves.

23 | Snakes are not deaf. They have no ears, but they can sense sounds. They have a thin plate of bone under their faces that helps them pick up sounds. First the bone senses the sound waves, and then it transfers the sound messages that it picks up to the snake's brain. Snakes can hear low sounds best. High noises are hard for them to pick up. They can also feel sound through the ground. Hearing isn't a snake's strongest sense, but snakes are able to _____.

                smell   see   hear

Snakes hear with a thin plate of

(a) skin.
(b) fat.
(c) muscle.
(d) bone.

24 | How is tea made? It isn't simply a matter of soaking a tea bag in hot water. That is how tea is brewed, and brewing is really the last step in the long process of making tea. The process begins in the Far East and India where tea plants are grown. When a tea plant is three to five years old, the leaves are ready to be picked. But tea leaves aren't ready for use just yet. They are sent to a factory. There the leaves are spread out on racks and dried. Then they are squeezed to remove any wetness. Next, the leaves are moved to another room where they are aged. Finally, they are dried one more time in an oven. Only after all these steps have been completed are the tea leaves ready for _____.

            eating   brewing   picking

Tea leaves are picked when the plant is

(a) three to five years old.
(b) twenty years old.
(c) one to two years old.
(d) eight years old.

25 | A smart farm woman invented a new way to wash clothes. Her husband was a dairyman. Every day he delivered milk all over the county. The milk was stored in large cans. On his route he drove over quite a few old dirt roads. It was a bumpy ride. This gave his wife an idea. When she wanted to do laundry she'd put the dirty clothes into a milk can with hot water and soap. Then her husband would put that can in his truck along with the cans filled with milk. The bumpy ride mixed up the clothes, water and soap. As the man drove, the clothes washed themselves _____.

               cheese   milky   clean

The farmer delivered

(a) laundry.
(b) milk.
(c) detergent.
(d) fertilizer.

26 | Eels are fish, but they look more like snakes. They live in fresh and salt water at different times in their lives. Young eels live in the fresh waters of lakes and rivers. But when it is time for them to mate and lay eggs, eels set off on a long journey. They travel thousands of miles to reach the middle of the Atlantic Ocean. Baby eels, called elvers, hatch from the eggs laid there. The older eels then stay in the ocean while the elvers swim to fresh water rivers and _____.

               oceans   lakes   seas

Baby eels are called

(a) worms.
(b) dwarfs.
(c) elvers.
(d) trolls.

27 | People invent new board games every year. But some games have been around for a long time. People were playing board games as long ago as 3000 B.C. That was the time of the ancient Egyptians. But the oldest game wasn't found in Egypt. It was dug up from the Royal Tombs of Ur. Ur was a city in a country that is now known as Iraq. The ancient board had twenty-six squares. It came with seven black and seven white counters. Experts think that it may have been the first backgammon game. The Ur backgammon didn't use dice as we know them today. Instead of being cubes, the dice were the same shape as the famous Egyptian _____.

        pharaohs   mummies   pyramids

Ur was a city in

(a) Israel.
(b) Iraq.
(c) Egypt.
(d) Iran.

28 | The cranium is part of the skull. The human skull has twenty-two bones. Eight of these bones enclose the brain. They make up the cranium. The other fourteen form the face and the jaw. Skull bones form a rigid, united structure in adults. In babies, the bones are soft in areas where the bones join. This allows the skull to grow. The cranium's thickness varies, but it averages a quarter of an inch. The cranium is thinnest near the temples. There it is only an eighth of an inch _____.

        thick   around   high

The number of bones that make up the cranium is

(a) eight.
(b) fourteen.
(c) twenty-two.
(d) thirty.

29 | Did you know that porpoises sleep with one eye open? They do this to keep from drowning in their sleep. Porpoises are mammals. This means that they need to breathe air. When awake, they surface every now and then to breathe. Of course, they must also breathe while they are asleep. So they must surface even in their sleep. However, if the ocean is rough and the porpoise goes up for air, it may take in water instead. That's why it keeps one eye open. It keeps track of the size of the _____.

        fish   **air**   **waves**

Porpoises surface in order to

(a) sleep.
(b) catch their food.
(c) drink fresh water.
(d) breathe.

30 | Your shoe size was determined by the length of barley grains. During the Middle Ages, the English king decreed that an inch would be the same length as three grains of barley. The average man back then had feet that were thirty-nine grains long. Shoe-makers called this standard size thirteen. A shoe that was one grain longer was size fourteen. Feet that were two grains longer than standard were size fifteen. For smaller feet, just subtract one grain at a time. Size twelve feet were thirty-eight grains long. This meant that a size six shoe was equal in length to thirty-two grains of _____.

        inches   **barley**   **feet**

The king declared that one inch equaled

(a) three barley grains.
(b) thirteen barley grains.
(c) thirty-nine barley grains.
(d) three hundred barley grains.

31 | A pirate once used wine jugs to escape from prison. His name was Bartolomo, and he was always robbing Spanish ships. Spanish sailors caught him many times, but they never could hang him. He was just too smart for them. Each time he was caught he managed to escape. He had only one weak point. He could not swim. The Spanish sailors finally learned of this. The next time they caught him they put him on a ship far out at sea. But soon he was on shore again, a free man. How had he done it? One night he escaped from his cell on the ship and went on deck. There he found two empty wine jugs. Knowing they would float, he dropped them into the water and then jumped quietly overboard himself. Using the jugs to help him float, he escaped to the shore and _____.

            boat   freedom   ship

Bartolomo used the wine jugs to help him

(a) float.
(b) get drunk.
(c) dive.
(d) sail.

32 | The Brazilian howler is a kind of monkey. It has a louder voice than most monkeys. This is because it has a very large bone at the base of its tongue. This bone acts as a kind of sounding box. It makes the monkey's voice deep and powerful. That's how the monkey got its name. People who live in or visit Brazil can hear a howler "sing." And sometimes a group of these monkeys will all howl _____.

            together   silently   bones

The howler is a type of

(a) bird.
(b) opera singer.
(c) insect.
(d) monkey.

33 | The capybara is the world's largest rodent. Squirrels, beavers and rats are rodents, too. But the capybara is larger than any of them. It grows to be four feet long. It can weigh one hundred pounds or more. Capybara live in South America. They look like big guinea pigs. They have rough, reddish-brown hair on their backs and yellow hair on their bellies. They have webbed feet for swimming. Jaguars like to kill and eat them. But capybaras are not hunters. They only eat _____.

                animals   plants   birds

Capybaras have webbed feet for

(a) digging.
(b) swimming.
(c) climbing.
(d) running.

34 | You can eat it and you can build with it. Does this sound like some miracle material? No, it's just rice. Farmers in Japan know how to get the most out of rice. Japan, along with China, grows much of the world's rice. Each kernel of rice is covered with a hull. The hulls used to be thrown away before the rice was sold. But farmers in Japan have found a use for the once useless hulls. They mix them into a kind of paste. The paste is formed into blocks which, when hard, become bricks. In Japan, buildings made with these bricks are called "houses of _____."

                wheat   rice   paper

Japanese farmers use the leftover rice hulls to make

(a) bricks.
(b) cereal.
(c) wood.
(d) glue.

35 | Some fashions are based on superstition. For instance, people in Sumatra think long hair brings good luck. Sumatra is an island in Indonesia. The weather there is hot and rainy. You might think that long hair would be too hot. But even the Sumatran men wear their hair long. They believe that their long hair helps their rice crops grow. Rice is the biggest food crop in Sumatra. It feeds most of the island people. So none of these men ever think of cutting their _____.

                hair   rice   crops

In Sumatra, men wear their hair

(a) short.
(b) long.
(c) curly.
(d) straight.

36 | The heart is a strong pump. It sends blood throughout the body. But the heart could not work without help from the brain. Part of the brain tells the heart how hard or fast to pump. The brain is also the center of learning. But long ago, people had it backwards. They thought that the heart was the center of intelligence. Egyptians would keep the heart of a dead king so that it would be ready for his next life. The brain, on the other hand, was thrown away. Its only role, they thought, was to fill the empty space inside the head. Although knowledge of the heart and brain has grown, people still use sayings from those ancient times. Surely you have heard memorizing called "learning by _____."

                mail   brain   heart

The heart of a dead Egyptian king was often

(a) pumped.
(b) kept.
(c) thrown away.
(d) studied.

37 | It takes more than wheels to make a roller skate roll. The wheels on roller skates move smoothly because they have little metal balls inside them. These balls are known as ball bearings. They fit in grooves between each wheel and its axle. They help reduce friction. Without them, the wheel and axle would scrape against each other. This scraping would slow down the wheel and the skates. Ball bearings move smoothly between the wheel and the axle to make the wheels turn easily. This helps people skate _____.

               faster   slowly   carefully

Ball bearings help to reduce

(a) speed.
(b) injuries.
(c) friction.
(d) weight.

38 | Some animals are hunters. Others are mainly prey. Some people say that the difference between the hunters and the hunted can be seen in their eyes. Where an animal's eyes are placed on its head shows its special needs. The tiger is a good example. Its eyes are close set on the front of its head. This allows the tiger to focus on its prey. In contrast, look at the eyes of a horse. A horse's eyes are on the sides of its head. The eyes can turn to allow the horse to see to the sides and partly behind itself. This helps the horse spot danger, so it can get away fast. Humans have forward-looking eyes. This theory suggests that people are natural _____.

               hunted   hunters   neutral

A tiger's eyes are set

(a) close together.
(b) far apart.
(c) on the back of its head.
(d) on the sides of its head.

39 | Bees don't sting unless they have to. They only sting to defend themselves. Worker bees have only one stinger. They can only sting once. They leave their stingers behind when they sting a person or an animal. The stinger keeps pumping poison into the wound. But the bee dies a few hours later. Queen bees can use their stingers many times. They only sting other queen bees, however. Drones, the male bees, don't have any stingers. They live short lives and never need to use a _____.

            stinger   bee   worker

Queen bees can use their stingers many times to sting

(a) people.
(b) animals.
(c) other queen bees.
(d) worker bees.

40 | Crowbars are used by firemen to pry open stuck doors. Builders may use crowbars to pry up shingles or floorboards. Do you know why this heavy-duty tool is named after a bird? It has to do with its shape. A crowbar is an iron bar that is a couple of feet long. It is about an inch thick. The bar's shape makes it a good lever. One end is curved like a fishhook. The other end is flattened and has a sharp edge that looks like a wedge. This shape reminded some people of the beak of a crow. They started calling the whole thing a crowbar. The name is still _____.

            wrong   used   changing

Crowbars are used mainly as

(a) hammers.
(b) scarecrows.
(c) saws.
(d) levers.

41 Many people in India live in mud houses. These people are so poor that they can't afford to build any other kind of house. Mud doesn't cost anything. The people take wet mud and pack it together. They make mud blocks and leave them to dry in the sun. The dried mud makes strong bricks. The people tie the mud blocks together with straw. Then, they build their homes with these blocks. There are a lot of poor people in India. So there are many parts of the country where whole villages are made of _____.

        mud   clay   straw

The people tie the mud bricks together with

(a) cement.
(b) straw.
(c) brick.
(d) glue.

42 The flounder is a type of flatfish. The odd thing about this fish is that both its eyes are on the same side of its head. Flounder are not born that way, though. When a flounder hatches, it looks like any other fish. As it grows, however, its body becomes flattened. One side of the fish is white and the other is a sandy color. The flounder lies on its white side on the ocean floor. Its sandy-colored side faces up. This makes the flounder blend in with the sand, so it can't be easily seen. For any other fish, this would cause a problem. One eye would be looking right into the sand. But nature has solved this problem for the flounder. As the fish grows, the eye on the bottom moves to the upper _____.

        sand   side   fish

Flounder are hard to see because they

(a) are almost blind.
(b) are extremely small.
(c) blend in with the sand.
(d) move very quickly.

43 | Strong winds once saved a man's life. Thomas Helms wanted to kill himself. He was twenty-seven years old and very depressed. He was an artist, and his work was not selling. So, a few days before Christmas, he decided to end his life. He went to the eighty-sixth floor of the Empire State Building. There, he climbed out of a window and tried to jump to his death. But a strong gust of wind blew him back inside the building. The force of nature saved Helms's _____.

death   life   wind

Thomas Helms wanted to jump out of the

(a) Statue of Liberty.
(b) Rockefeller Center.
(c) World Trade Center.
(d) Empire State Building.

44 | Birds build nests in many different types of places. They build them close to their food supply. For example, ocean birds find their food out at sea. They build their nests in the reeds and grasses of the seashore. One bird that chooses odd nesting sites is the house wren. This small bird eats insects found on the ground. Its favorite nesting site is in a birdhouse made by people. If it can't find a house already made, it will use a hole in the ground, an old tin can, an old hat or even a scarecrow's pocket. One woman has an interesting story about a wren. She hung her husband's fishing pants out on the line to dry. When she started to take the pants off the line, she saw that a wren had built a nest in the pocket of the _____.

shirt   pants   nest

One woman found a wren's nest in

(a) a scarecrow's pocket.
(b) the pocket of a pair of fishing pants.
(c) a birdhouse made by her husband.
(d) the reeds and grasses near the seashore.

45 | Most birds sleep in trees. But they don't fall from their branches while they are asleep. This is because birds have tendons in their legs that lock them in place on tree branches. These tendons run from the toes through the ankle and legs. They attach to the muscles above the leg. When a bird lands on a twig, this whole system goes to work. The ankle joint bends under the bird's weight. This bending pulls the tendon back. The tendon, in turn, pulls on the bird's toes, forcing them to curl around the perch. This gives the bird a firm grip so that it can safely _____.

          fly   sleep   eat

The bird's special tendon is connected to its

(a) neck.
(b) wings.
(c) beak.
(d) toes.

46 | Peanuts are the fruit of the peanut plant. They are really a kind of pea, not a nut. Peanut plants, like other peas, grow seeds inside pods. The seeds are the peanuts. The pods are the shells. They are different from other pea plants because their pods grow underground. Stems grow down from the plant into the ground. The peanuts grow on the buried ends of these stems. These buried pea pods have given peanuts some other names. They are often called groundnuts, goobers, goober peas, or groundpeas. Whatever name people use, peanuts are a healthy and tasty _____.

          food   branch   pod

The pea pods of peanut plants grow

(a) above ground.
(b) underground.
(c) underwater.
(d) in sunlight.

47 | There is no such thing as a cat with a sweet tooth. Cats can't taste sugar. Human taste buds can tell the difference between four basic flavors. People can taste sweet, salty, bitter, and sour flavors with their tongues. But cats don't have taste buds for sweet things. Humans can have cravings for sweets. People get rotten teeth and gain weight from eating too much sugar. But cats never have these problems. They just can't tell if something is sweet or _____.

        human   not   sweet

Cats cannot taste

(a) salt.
(b) sour.
(c) sweet.
(d) bitter.

48 | Which would you rather do, climb a mountain or travel from one country to another? Well, there's one place where you can do both at the same time. It's Mont Blanc. Mont Blanc is a mountain in the Alps. Its peak is the highest point in the mountain range. Part of the Alps is in France, and part is in southern Italy. Mont Blanc lies along the border between France and Italy. The border divides the mountain almost exactly in half. The peak, however, is in France. Mont Blanc means "white mountain" in French. And Mont Blanc does look white. About forty square miles of the mountain is covered by a glacier. The mountain got its name from this thick layer of _____.

        ice   France   range

In which two countries does Mont Blanc lie?

(a) Italy and Spain
(b) France and the United States
(c) Italy and France
(d) France and the Alps

49 | Burns Blintliff sells mud for a living. He sells it to major league baseball teams. They use it to get their baseballs ready for games. New baseballs are slick and slippery. This makes it hard for pitchers to get a good grip and control their throws. So Blintliff's mud is useful. Baseballs are rubbed with this mud before they are used in games. The mud makes the balls easier to handle. Blintliff has a secret supply of mud. He doesn't tell anyone where it comes from. That is strictly his own _____.

        team   business   slippery

Baseballs are rubbed with Blintliff's mud

(a) after they have been hit.
(b) before they are used in the game.
(c) after the game is over.
(d) while the game is in progress.

50 | There is a lot of life on the seashore. Ocean water collects in little pools among the rocks at low tide. Some people call them tidal pools, and others call them rock pools. The pools are sheltered from waves. They also tend to be warmer than the nearby ocean. Lots of sea animals live in these pools. Hermit crabs, which live in the old shells of other shellfish, find plenty of shells in the pools. Starfish like tidal pools, as well. The water is calm and there are rocks to rest on. There are many other creatures in rock pools. Sometimes it is easier to find them in rock pools than in the _____.

        ocean   sand   shower

Rock pools form when

(a) there is a storm.
(b) the tide is low.
(c) the tide is rising.
(d) people build sand castles on the beach.

51 There is a killer crab in the Pacific. It's called the giant spider crab. This crab can be up to three feet tall and weigh more than thirty pounds. With its legs spread out, it covers an area twelve feet across. Its huge claws are strong enough to rip off a human arm. This creature lives only in Japanese waters. It takes several people to capture one. First they catch it in large nets. Then they bring it ashore and hold it to the ground until it stops struggling. They catch this crab because it is a valuable source of _____.

        amusement   food   claws

The giant spider crab lives

(a) in very deep waters.
(b) off the coast of Japan.
(c) off the coast of America.
(d) in the Atlantic Ocean.

52 You'll never see a flying fish flap its wings. To begin with, flying fish don't really have wings. They have fins, like other types of fish. But flying fish can spread their fins. They use them to glide through the air. Flying fish can glide great distances at high speeds. They can travel at a rate of twenty to thirty miles per hour. They can cover several hundred yards in one flight. Whether one of these fish has a good or a bad glide depends on its takeoff. The flying fish throws itself from the water by pushing with its powerful tail. Once the fish is in the air, it spreads out its fins and _____.

        swims   glides   runs

The flying fish pushes itself out of the water by using its

(a) tail.
(b) wingspan.
(c) wings.
(d) fins.

53 Glowworms glow in the dark. They have chemicals in their bodies that make a greenish light. There are different types of glowworms. They are the larvae of different kinds of insects. A larva is the first stage of an insect. It looks like a worm and has not yet grown wings. One type of glowworm lives in dark caves on New Zealand's North Island. They are the larvae of fungus gnats. New Zealand glowworms make webs that glow in the dark. These webs hang from the ceilings of the caves. They give off enough light to brighten the caves. Glowworms spin these light webs to attract flies. The glowworms eat the flies that get caught in their _____.

          flies   wings   webs

Glowworms in New Zealand spin webs to

(a) light the caves.
(b) catch flies.
(c) grow fungus.
(d) grow wings.

54 Tin has been a useful metal for centuries. It can be combined with copper to make bronze. It is shiny and will not tarnish or blacken as silver does. Also, tin is much cheaper than many other metals. It does not rust like steel or iron. For this reason, some food cans are coated with a thin layer of tin. The cans couldn't be made of solid tin. Tin is very soft and bends easily. Many cans are made from sheets of iron or steel. The sheets are then coated with tin. This metal gives the can its shiny look and also keeps the iron or steel from _____.

          bending   melting   rusting

Food tins are not made of solid tin because tin is

(a) soft and bends easily.
(b) a metal that tarnishes.
(c) found in copper.
(d) much too expensive.

55 | Hippopotamuses sometimes seem to sweat blood. But the sweat isn't really blood. In fact, it is good for the hippo. Hippos have tough, thick skin. If they are away from water for too long, their skin starts to dry and crack. To stop this, the hippo's skin gives off a reddish substance. This sweat is oily and thick and gathers in droplets. It helps keep the skin from cracking. The sweat also oozes out when hippos are hot, excited or in pain. It is an important form of _____.

        skin   blood   protection

The hippo's sweat keeps its skin

(a) moist.
(b) dry.
(c) bleeding.
(d) white.

56 | Most fish eat other, smaller fish. Some fish have special ways to catch their food. The swordfish and the sawfish, for instance, both have long noses. They use them to stun smaller fish so that they can eat them. The manta uses its strong, winglike fins to stun its prey. The thresher shark has a tail that is as long as the rest of its body. The edge of this shark's tail is so sharp that it can cut like a knife. It kills its victims by slashing them to death. The stingray uses a poison dagger in its tail to catch fish. The torpedo fish gives its victims an electric shock. These fish prove that the best fishermen are found in the _____.

        water   air   jungle

The thresher shark uses its sharp tail to

(a) attract other fish.
(b) cut other fish.
(c) shock other fish.
(d) poison other fish.

57 | Different kinds of snakes have their own ways of catching food, but they all eat and swallow the same way. A constrictor snake slowly squeezes an animal to death and then eats it. Other snakes may use poison to kill their prey. Some snakes catch flies with their tongues. And some just grab their prey with their teeth and swallow it. Snakes can't chew their food. They have to swallow it whole. Their teeth are sharp and shaped like needles. But they curve inward, toward their throats. These teeth help snakes get a good grip to force their food toward their _____.

          stomachs   mouths   prey

Snakes' teeth are shaped like

(a) needles.
(b) blocks.
(c) balls.
(d) stones.

58 | What do tree roots do? They hold trees firmly in the earth. They also provide trees with minerals and water. A tree's roots absorb water and minerals from the ground. Then the tree uses the water and minerals to make food. It gathers sunlight through its leaves. The tree mixes all these things together to feed itself. It could not make food without the sunlight that it takes in through its leaves, or the water and minerals from its _____.

          leaves   food   roots

Trees use their roots to absorb minerals and

(a) sunlight.
(b) water.
(c) air.
(d) rocks.

59 It can be hard for young birds to survive. They may be eaten by animals. They can fall out of their nests and break their necks. But the biggest threat to their safety is rain. Rain makes it hard for the adult birds to find food. This means that they have to spend more time away from the nest while they hunt. While the parents are away, the baby birds may freeze in the cold rain. A long rain storm once wiped out all the baby terns in the state of Maine. But the adult birds can't stay in the nests to protect the baby birds. They have to go find food, or else the chicks will _____.

            fly   sing   starve

Baby birds sometimes die from freezing in the

(a) food.
(b) rain.
(c) dark.
(d) hunt.

60 Different animals keep cool in different ways. For instance, humans sweat, and dogs and cats pant. These are two ways to release heat. Birds use a different method. They are very active and can build up a lot of heat in a short time. So when they fly they breathe in a great deal of air. Birds use at least half of this air to cool their bodies. The other half puts oxygen in their blood. Some birds, such as the pigeon, use only one-quarter of the air they breathe for oxygen. The other three-quarters helps them keep cool. So, a bird's breathing system actually serves two different _____.

            airs   purposes   breaths

The pigeon uses one-quarter of the air it breathes for

(a) cooling off.
(b) flying.
(c) oxygen.
(d) food.

61 | The wolf's cry in the wild sounds full of loneliness. In fact though, wolves use their howls and calls as signals among themselves. Wolves have strong family ties. Many mate for life. Both parents feed and train their wolf pups. The families stay together for a long time. Most wolf packs are just family groups. Because most wolves rely on their packs for food, shelter and companionship, they have developed a system of signals to keep the pack _____.

               lost   separate   together

Most wolf packs are

(a) quickly disbanded.
(b) lost in the wilderness.
(c) formed for fighting.
(d) family groups.

62 | Reptiles were the first animals to live on land. Some of them later took to the air. The first birds were a type of reptile. Birds and reptiles such as snakes, lizards and turtles are the same in many ways. Most birds and reptiles lay eggs. Experts think that feathers are a form of reptile scales. Ancient birds looked like feathered lizards. They had fingers on their wings for climbing trees. They also had long tails with feathers on each side. Some had teeth inside their long beaks. Birds have changed a lot since then. Although they are distantly related, modern birds and reptiles do not look much _____.

             together   **different**   **alike**

Experts think that bird feathers are a form of reptile

(a) scales.
(b) teeth.
(c) wings.
(d) beaks.

63 | The archaeopteryx (ARE-key-OP-tuh-riks) lived 125 million years ago. Experts think it was the first bird. They have found fossils of it in Bavaria. Its name means "ancient one with wings." Some younger bird fossils have been found in America. These birds lived 70 million years ago. The ichthyornis (IK-thee-OR-nuhs) is one of these. Its name means "fish bird." It looked like a small gull with strong wings. The hesperornis (HES-puh-ROR-nuhs) lived around the same time. Its name means "bird of the west." This bird looked like a large loon with teeth. It was six feet tall. There are very few birds this big on earth _____.

        today   tomorrow   yesterday

The archaeopteryx lived

(a) 70 million years ago.
(b) 125 million years ago.
(c) 17 million years ago.
(d) 625 million years ago.

64 | Ducks spend most of their lives in water. Their bodies are well built for swimming and fishing. Ducks have short wings so they can dive underwater. They have long necks for catching food. Their webbed feet make good paddles for swimming. And although ducks live in water, they don't get very wet. Ducks have natural waterproofing. They have a gland under their tails that gives off a waxy oil. Ducks rub this oil over their feathers with their bills. Water just rolls off a duck's waterproof _____.

        feet   feathers   bills

Ducks waterproof their feathers with

(a) webbed feet.
(b) tail feathers.
(c) waxy oil.
(d) long necks.

65 | Earth was once an impossible place to live. About 4,600 million years ago, it was a liquid, molten mass. Its temperature was about 7,232 degrees Fahrenheit. That is much too hot for any form of life that is on earth now. At that time, all the heavy elements, such as iron, sank. They formed the center of the earth. The earth slowly cooled. When it reached 1,832 degrees, a crust of islands began to form. Clouds of gases formed in the atmosphere. They included methane, ammonia and water vapor. We could not live if we had to breathe such air. These gases also cooled in time. Then it began to rain. It rained for thousands of years. This rain cooled the earth. It also helped to form the _____.

        moon   mountains   oceans

The center of the earth is made of

(a) gases.
(b) heavy elements.
(c) methane and ammonia.
(d) thick vapors.

66 | Many people don't like having to drive in the rain or at night. They must not know that bad weather can be good for a car. Engines run best when the weather is wet and the skies are dark. You see, engines need cool air to run smoothly. Both nights and rainy days provide cool air. Cooler air is denser, or heavier, than warm air. So when it is cool outside, an engine takes in more air. More air in the engine brings more power. More air also prevents engine knock. This is the sound of a poorly running _____.

        driver   engine   weather

Cooler air is

(a) thinner.
(b) denser.
(c) drier.
(d) warmer.

67 | Would you know quicksilver if you saw it? Chances are you have seen it many times. But you probably didn't know it by that name. Quicksilver is a silvery metal. But it is not like most metals. For one thing, it is liquid. Its name tells something else about it. No, the *quick* doesn't mean that it is speedy. Long ago, *quick* meant "living." When quicksilver is poured, it breaks up into little drops. It seems to have a life of its own. This unusual metal was found to be useful. It reacts quickly to small changes in temperature. As it gets hotter, it expands. As it gets cooler, it contracts. It is often used in thermometers to record the temperature. This odd liquid metal is also known as _____.

        silver   mercury   metal

Quicksilver reacts to changes in

(a) pressure.
(b) temperature.
(c) wind speed.
(d) motion.

68 | The human tongue can taste four basic flavors. These are sweet, sour, salty and bitter. Tongues have taste buds on the front, sides and back. Taste buds react to chemicals in food. They send signals to the brain, and the brain sorts out the signals. This is how people can tell how foods taste. Most taste buds react to more than one flavor. Some taste buds can sense two tastes, such as sweet and sour. Others can react to three or four tastes at the same _____.

        sweet   time   salt

Tongues have taste buds on the front, sides and

(a) top.
(b) back.
(c) bottom.
(d) middle.

69 | Have you ever heard someone say, "I'm as mad as a hornet"? This may give you the idea that hornets are always angry. Well, that's not quite true. Hornets are usually calm insects. They spend most of their day working together. They chew wood and use it to build their nest. They gather food for the queen and young hornets. They don't have time to get angry at people. But hornets are quick to sting anyone who bothers the nest. Their sting is very painful. That may be why people think of hornets as mean. But these stinging insects are really just protecting their _____.

        home   flowers   toys

Hornets sting only when

(a) they are angry.
(b) a person or animal bothers their nest.
(c) they are near death.
(d) a person tries to feed them.

70 | How can you tell where a penny comes from? You can find out just by looking at it. In the United States, coins are made in mints. The mints stamp the coins out of pieces of metal. There are three mints. The main mint is in Philadelphia. The other two are in Denver and San Francisco. Many coins have little marks to show where they were made. It's really quite an easy code to break. Pennies that were minted in Denver have a small *D* printed below the date. Coins from San Francisco have an *S* in the same spot. But if the coin was made in Philadelphia, there will be no _____.

        money   value   mark

The main United States mint is in

(a) Denver.
(b) San Francisco.
(c) Washington, D.C.
(d) Philadelphia.

71 What are animals doing in the stock market? Stockbrokers sometimes talk about "bull" and "bear" markets. But you won't find animals in the New York Stock Exchange. Bull and bear are terms that stock experts use. They stand for certain ways of trading stocks. Bulls are brokers who buy stocks that they don't plan to keep for very long. They hold them only until the price goes up. They try to sell the stocks for a profit. Bears, on the other hand, sell their stocks as the price is going down. They hope to buy them back when the price is even lower. Bear and bull brokers can cause quite a fuss in the stock market. However, they probably wouldn't cause as much trouble as the real _____.

        brokers   prices   animals

A bear sells when the prices are

(a) going up.
(b) going down.
(c) being changed.
(d) staying the same.

72 Have you ever seen a robin bend its head to the ground? Some people think that when a robin does this it is listening for worms. Well, this isn't quite true. The robin is worm hunting. But robins don't listen for worms, they look for them. Birds can see better if they focus only one eye at a time on something. The robin tilts its head down to point one eye at the ground. Why do robins look for worms rather than listen for them? For one thing, birds can see much better than they can hear. In fact, they can see far better than people can. But there's another reason—earthworms make very little _____.

        noise   food   sight

A robin tilts its head in order to

(a) listen for earthworms.
(b) clean its feathers.
(c) focus one eye on the ground.
(d) use its beak to probe for worms.

73 | The children of Persian princes were always given a good education. When they were just babies, a prince's children were put in the charge of special tutors. At age seven they were taught to ride a horse. Then, at fourteen they were brought to the magi. These were priests who were respected for their wisdom. With the magi, the children went through four stages of learning. At each stage, they were taught by a different magus. The first taught the ways of the priesthood. The second preached the value of truth. The third taught them courage and strength. And the fourth taught them how to rule their emotions. Of all the tasks, the last was probably the most _____.

        difficult   expensive   childish

At age seven, a prince's children learned

(a) to ride a horse.
(b) the value of truth.
(c) to be brave and strong.
(d) to rule their emotions.

74 | Woodpeckers peck holes in trees to get food. These birds have strong, sharp beaks that they use to drill into the trees. Their feet help them cling to the sides of tree trunks and branches. Two of their toes point forward, and two point backward to help them keep their balance. Their stiff tail feathers also push against the trunks to help the birds hold onto the trees. After a woodpecker has drilled into a tree, it sticks its tongue in the hole. These birds have sticky tongues with sharp barbs on the tips. They use the barbs to spear insects that live in the wood, or they catch bugs with the sticky sides of their _____.

        tongues   beaks   feathers

Woodpeckers use their beaks to

(a) drill holes in trees.
(b) spear insects.
(c) cling to tree trunks.
(d) balance on steep trunks.

75 | Birds have to eat a lot of food. In fact, they eat all day long. Their stomachs are very small, so they must spread their meals out through the day. But some birds, such as the bobwhite, can eat only at certain times during the day. They eat two heavy meals each day. Because their stomachs are tiny, they have to store most of the food after they eat it. So, halfway between their mouths and stomachs, they have an organ called a crop. It does not break down the food, as the stomach does. It just keeps it in storage. When the stomach is ready for more food, the crop sends some of the stored food to the stomach for _____.

        digestion   eating   drinking

The bird's crop is used for

(a) breathing.
(b) digestion.
(c) sleeping.
(d) storage.

76 | Have you ever tried to walk on stilts? It's not easy. Stilts are long, strong pieces of wood. They have blocks part way up for you to put your feet on. You hold on to the upper ends of the stilts as you walk. Some stilts don't come up high enough to hold on to. These are made to be strapped to the walker's legs. Such stilts are harder to use. It's more difficult to stay balanced on them. Some circus performers use this type of stilt. They often dress as Uncle Sam, with a top hat, a blue coat, and long striped pants covering the stilts. Eddy Wolf of Loyal, Wisconsin, walked on the world's highest stilts. The stilts measured more than forty feet from his ankles to the _____.

        sky   feet   ground

The stilts that are hardest to use are strapped to a person's

(a) head.
(b) arms.
(c) pants.
(d) legs.

77 | There is a custom in Italy that a person should not kill a snake unless the moon is full. What has the full moon got to do with snakes? The people believe that when there is a full moon all the snakes get drunk on the grapes in the vineyards. A vineyard is an area where grapes are grown. There are many in Italy. The grapes are used to make wine. People believe that when the snakes are drunk it is all right to kill them. But at any other time killing a snake is said to bring bad luck to a family. So, for most of each month, the snakes in Italy are _____.

        afraid   killed   safe

In Italy, some people believe that snakes should only be killed when

(a) they are sober.
(b) the moon is not full.
(c) the moon is full.
(d) the grapes are ripe.

78 | Clothes don't last long when kids are wearing them. Active children can really destroy their clothes, with dirt, rips and general hard wear. Children tend to wear holes in the knees of their pants. A new pair of jeans can look old after one day of playing. Mending the pants can take a lot of time. What's more, the repairs don't always last. But some parents have found a way to make the knees in a pair of pants last longer. They "repair" the pants as soon as they buy them. They put iron-on patches on the inside of both knees. These patches reinforce the cloth, so the knees last for a while before they need _____.

        tearing   mending   wearing

Children often tear their pants at the

(a) belt.
(b) flies.
(c) knees.
(d) cuffs.

79 | A thief once lost money when he robbed a store. How can you steal and not gain anything? Well, in 1977 a supermarket in England was robbed. The thief had come up with his own way of robbing. First he filled a basket with groceries. He then took it to the checkout counter and put a ten-pound note down. The clerk picked up the bill and opened the cash register. The thief grabbed all the money and ran. Most store owners would be upset if their shop were robbed. But in this case the owner probably didn't mind much. There had been only 4.37 pounds in the register. The store still had the thief's ten-pound note. The thief had lost 5.63 pounds on the _____.

        robbery   note   owner

The note the thief put on the counter was worth

(a) five pounds.
(b) fifteen pounds.
(c) 4.37 pounds.
(d) ten pounds.

80 | The flavor of food is the result of both tasting and smelling. Taste buds on the tongue sense basic flavors. They tell you if a food is salty, sweet, bitter or sour. That is all they can do. But the exact flavors of foods go beyond just these four tastes. We know that there are many more than four flavors. Much of what we know of tastes comes from our sense of smell. We smell the special flavors of each food. Many people notice that they can't taste food when they have head colds. This is because a stuffy nose keeps them from smelling the food they eat. Some foods have no flavor without their smell. Coffee and chocolate both get most of their flavor from their _____.

        scent   taste   texture

The flavor of food comes from its taste and its

(a) heat.
(b) taste.
(c) flavor.
(d) smell.

81 | Do you know someone who saves everything? Gum wrappers? Empty shopping bags? People like this are often nicknamed pack rats. There is a real rodent called a pack rat that saves almost everything, too. If one gets into a house, it will take objects that catch its eye. Bright things such as coins and eyeglasses are popular with pack rats. Sometimes pack rats are called trade rats. That's because they often leave something behind when they pick up a new object. Pack rats look like regular rats. But they have furry tails instead of hairless ones. Pack rats also tend to be cleaner than other rats. They will not live in sewers or garbage dumps. Native to North America, pack rats live in nests on mountain ledges or in _____.

                dumps   boats   bushes

Pack rats especially like

(a) clothing.
(b) paper money.
(c) bright objects.
(d) acorns.

82 | What is the largest fish in the world? Although many people may think it's the whale, they are wrong. A whale is not a fish. Whales, like dolphins, are ocean mammals. The biggest fish in the ocean is called the whale shark. The largest whale shark ever found was caught in 1919. It weighed about ninety thousand pounds and was a little more than sixty feet long. Whale sharks are rare fish. They are found only in the warmer areas of the ocean. Swimmers don't have to worry about whale sharks. They are harmless to humans and to other fish. They eat only small _____.

                fish   plants   sharks

The whale shark is a type of

(a) fish.
(b) mammal.
(c) plant.
(d) ocean.

83 | People normally chew only when they are eating. But one man chewed his way out of jail. Hans Schaarschmidt was in jail for robbery. He was supposed to stay there for six years. But the jail he was staying in was too old to hold him. There were wooden bars across his window. The wood was rotten. So Schaarschmidt decided to chew through them. Every day he chewed until his teeth were sore. Then he covered up the place where he had chewed the wood with some partly-chewed bread. In three months he chewed a hole large enough for him to fit through. Then he escaped. But three weeks later he was captured and put back in jail. He was put in another jail the second time. His cell had windows with iron, not wooden, _____.

           holes   bread   bars

Schaarschmidt chewed his way out of

(a) court.
(b) jail.
(c) bread.
(d) home.

84 | Do you like shrimp cocktail? Do you really know what a shrimp is? This sea animal has five pairs of legs joined to its body, as do lobsters and crabs. It is a close relative of these animals. Shrimp grow up to nine inches long. Larger shrimp are sometimes called prawns. Shrimp swim backwards, using their fan-shaped tails. They don't swim forward. They live in both the Atlantic and Pacific Oceans, near coastlines. Large shrimp are caught and sold at fish markets. As with crabs and lobsters, many types of shrimp can be _____.

           cocktail   eaten   seen

The name for a large shrimp is

(a) midget.
(b) lobster.
(c) crab.
(d) prawn.

85 | What does a bar of iron have in common with a twinkling star? Well, you may have seen pictures of iron being heated in a fire. At first the metal becomes a very dull red. As it gets hotter it gets redder. Soon it is bright red. If kept in the fire even longer, it will become a brilliant white. The same thing happens with stars. A star's color depends on its temperature. The coldest stars are dull red. The very hottest stars all shine with a color that is bluish-_____.

        green   red   white

The color of a star is related to its

(a) size.
(b) distance.
(c) temperature.
(d) location.

86 | Many frogs live on land. But that doesn't mean they can live very far from water. Although frogs spend much of their time on land, they must stay close to water all of their lives. All frogs are born in water. When they are young, they are called tadpoles. Tadpoles are really more like fish than frogs. They have long tails and gills for breathing air from the water. But tadpoles don't stay that way for very long. As they grow, their tails slowly disappear. Legs grow from their bodies. The gills develop into lungs so that the young frogs can breathe directly from the air. Now they are ready to climb onto land for the first time. Frogs can stay on land as long as their skin remains _____.

        dry   green   wet

A tadpole has a long tail and

(a) legs.
(b) lungs.
(c) gills.
(d) fish.

87 | Out on the prairies, rattlesnakes sometimes crawl into tents and sleeping bags. They aren't looking for a fight. They're just looking for a warm place to spend the night. Snakes are cold-blooded animals. This means that their body temperature is the same temperature as the air around them. So, they look for warm places to rest. Some people are used to this habit of rattlesnakes. They can sleep all night with a snake in their tents. These brave campers just curl up in their bags and try not to roll over onto the snake. The rattlesnake leaves again as soon as the sun _____.

                  sets   rises   falls

Rattlesnakes like to sleep in places that are

(a) cold.
(b) warm.
(c) soft.
(d) crowded.

88 | What's on your mind? Your pupils may let people know. Pupils are the openings in the eyes. They let in light to allow you to see. When you are in a bright room, your pupils get smaller. This is because there's plenty of light. At night, or when you enter a dark room, your pupils get larger. This is to let as much light as possible into your eyes. Experts say that other things besides light will change the size of the pupils. If you like what you see, then your pupils tend to get bigger. If not, they shrink. Good poker players have known this fact for a while. That's why when they play they often wear eyeshades. If they get a bad hand, other players won't see their pupils _____.

                shrink   grow   darken

In dark rooms your pupils get

(a) bigger.
(b) smaller.
(c) heavier.
(d) darker.

89 Do you know that flies can't eat? Their mouths are made only to suck liquids. Like all insects, flies go through three stages as they grow. First they are larva, then pupa, and, finally, adults. Fly larva are called maggots. Maggots eat all the time, and they grow bigger and bigger. When they are big enough, they spin cocoons. This is the pupa stage. Inside the cocoons, they grow wings and turn into adults. Once flies reach the adult stage, they never eat again. They just take in _____.

                maggots   liquids   food

Fly larva are called

(a) pupa.
(b) adults.
(c) cocoons.
(d) maggots.

90 Have you ever tried to write a sentence without an *e* in it? Ernest Vincent Wright, a man whose name has three *e*'s, wrote a novel that has only one *e* in it. The book is 50,110 words long. It is called *Gadsby*. In order to keep from using an *e*, Wright tied down that key on his typewriter. The book is about a man named John Gadsby who tries to make his hometown more progressive. Wright said that his greatest problems were avoiding words such as *he*, *she* and *they*. He also found it hard not to use verbs that ended in *-ed*. It took Wright 165 days to write *Gadsby*. He wrote it only to show that it was possible to write without *e*'s. He died at the age of sixty-seven, on the day the book was released. Today you would have to pay $1,000 for a copy of _____.

                Wright   novels   *Gadsby*

How many *e*'s does *Gadsby* contain?

(a) 165
(b) 1
(c) 50,110
(d) 1,000

91 | Movies are one of the most popular forms of entertainment. They take us to places we may never go. They tell stories that make us laugh or cry. They can make us angry or thoughtful. But movies have not always done these things. The first movies didn't have any sound. They didn't even have any stories to tell! Still, great numbers of people went to see them. The movies were only minutes long. They showed such things as a train moving down a track, men fighting, or couples dancing. People were just amazed to see pictures that moved. The first time a movie had a story was in 1903. It was called *The Life of an American Fireman.* It was made by a man named Edwin Porter. The business of making movies continued to grow with great speed. It seemed that everyone in America was making movies. It was a business that was new and _____.

exciting   sad   dull

The Life of an American Fireman was the first movie to have

(a) a story.
(b) sound.
(c) color.
(d) actors.

92 | Some gouramis (goo-RAH-mees) are called kissing fish. Gouramis are a type of tropical fish. They first came from Asia. People like to keep these fish for their pretty colors. Gouramis also have an interesting habit. They touch each other with their mouths. To humans, this looks like kissing. Scientists have tried to find out why these fish "kiss." But so far they have not found any _____.

fish   answers   kisses

Gouramis are a type of tropical

(a) fish.
(b) snake.
(c) bird.
(d) moth.

93 | The Hope diamond is the largest blue diamond in the world. It is worth a great deal of money, but you might not want to own it. It is said that a curse haunts the owner of this gem. Five hundred years ago, a Hindu priest stole it from the forehead of an idol in a temple. The priest was killed for his crime. A Frenchman who later owned the diamond was killed by wild dogs. Then the French royal family got the Hope diamond. Princess de Lamballe was beaten to death by a mob. Marie Antoinette was beheaded. The diamond's next owner, Jacques Celot, killed himself. A Russian owner gave it to his mistress, then he murdered her. Later Thomas Henry Hope bought the diamond. He, however, had no ill luck. The diamond was finally bought by the Smithsonian Institution in Washington, D.C. And there ends the _____.

        diamond   curse   crimes

Princess de Lamballe was beaten to death by

(a) the French royal family.
(b) her husband.
(c) an angry mob.
(d) a Hindu priest.

94 | Have you ever wondered where all the salt in the sea came from? If you have, then you are not alone. Scientists have been trying to figure this out, as well. No one knows the answer for sure. Even scientists can only make a good guess. A guess that is based on facts is called a theory. Here is one theory about sea salt. Long ago the earth was dry. Many of the rocks contained salt, which is a mineral. Then the oceans were formed by heavy rains that fell for a long time. The rains washed salt off the rocks of the earth. The salt was washed into the oceans as they were being made. After a time, the oceans were full of salt. Today there is about a quarter of a pound of salt in every gallon of sea _____.

        rocks   water   earth

According to one theory, sea salt came from

(a) ancient oceans.
(b) rain.
(c) mines.
(d) rocks.

95 | Many people are confused by cobwebs. What makes them? Are they only dust, or are they webs made by insects called cobs? If you think they are made by cobs, you are almost right. The word *cobweb* comes from an Old English word, *coppeweb*. The word *coppe* (CAHP-uh) means spider. Spiders make long threads and weave them into webs. Dust collects on the webs that are no longer used. People often call these dusty webs cobwebs. You can see how the word *coppeweb* became *cobweb*. Try saying *coppeweb* a few times. You can hear how the word *coppe* became _____.

        cob   spider   dust

The Old English word *coppe* means

(a) insect.
(b) web.
(c) spider.
(d) dust.

96 | Every parent would love a dog like Ringo. Ringo was a Saint Bernard. He lived with the Saleh family in Euless, Texas. The family included a two-year-old boy named Randy. Randy and Ringo were always together. Ringo kept an eye on the boy. One day Randy wandered away from home. The police searched for him for two hours with no luck. But the boy was safe with Ringo. Ringo did cause a traffic jam, though. Randy had gone out into the middle of a busy road to play. To protect him, Ringo sat down right in front of the boy. He wouldn't budge. He tried to nudge Randy to the side of the road. But the boy thought that the dog was just playing. So he went right back into the road. Ringo was getting upset. Finally, Harley Jones, who had gotten caught in the traffic jam, calmed the dog. Still, Ringo would not move until Randy was _____.

        happy   safe   afraid

Ringo protected Randy by

(a) sitting in front of him in the road.
(b) going to get Harley Jones.
(c) pulling him out of the road.
(d) barking at the cars on the road.

97 | A Greek myth tells of a slave who predicted the downfall of a king. The story takes place on the island of Samos. The king, Ancaeus, was the son of Zeus, who was king of the gods. Ancaeus had just had a great vineyard planted. His slaves had been forced to work long and hard to plant the grapes. One slave told the ruler that he would never live to taste the wine made from his grapes. The king scoffed at the slave's prediction. When at last the wine had been made, the king sent for the slave. "What do you think of your prophecy now?" said the king. "There is many a slip between the cup and the lip," replied the slave. Scarcely had he heard this when Ancaeus was told that a wild boar was destroying his vineyard. The king set down his cup of untasted wine and went out to drive the animal away. But the boar charged him and Ancaeus was _____.

        saved   frightened   killed

Ancaeus was killed by a

(a) slave.
(b) king.
(c) god.
(d) boar.

98 | A punt is not only the act of kicking a football while it's in the air. It's also a part of a wine bottle. It is a dent in the bottom of the bottle. Most good wine bottles have punts. They serve two purposes. First, they trap sediments. These are particles in the wine that settle to the bottom. In a good wine bottle, the sediments will stick to the punt instead of pouring with the wine. Second, punts help to improve the strength of the _____.

        bottle   wine   cork

One purpose of a punt is to

(a) sweeten the wine.
(b) strengthen the wine bottle.
(c) stir up the sediment.
(d) age the wine.

99 | It is often said that dog is man's best friend. Stevie Wilson and his father would no doubt agree. One winter day, Stevie's father was outside trying to saddle a horse. Three-year-old Stevie strayed out onto a frozen lake with his dog Taffy. The ice wasn't very thick. Stevie fell through into the freezing cold water. Taffy raced to the corral where Mr. Wilson was riding. The cocker spaniel ran around the corral barking. But the man paid no attention. Taffy ran back to the lake. Then she raced back and nipped Mr. Wilson's horse. The horse almost threw its rider. This time Mr. Wilson got the message. He followed the dog onto the lake. He saw his son's coat on the surface of the water. He jumped into the lake and saved the boy. Six hours later, when Stevie woke up, the first thing he saw was _____ .

            Taffy   ice   horses

Taffy was a

(a) hound.
(b) horse.
(c) terrier.
(d) cocker spaniel.

100 | Not all plants need soil to grow. And not all plants have stems and leaves. Some plants sprout in jars of jam or on leftover food. Such plants grow on their own, often when and where you don't want them to. These plants are called molds. Molds, like mushrooms, are members of the fungus family. Most molds look like fuzz. They feed on the sugar that is in foods. Molds will often spoil a food's taste. Sometimes they can even be dangerous to your _____ .

            health   plants   fungus

Mold is a kind of

(a) mushroom.
(b) jam.
(c) sugar.
(d) fungus.